SPRING NEXT GENERATION

THINKING IN OBJECTS

J. Scott Stanlick

DEDICATION

I dedicate this book to my best friend Jamie Kay.

Table of Contents

ACKNOWLEDGMENTS

A huge shout out to all the awesome and beautiful people who work tirelessly to provide wicked cool open-source software for free of charge! I make a living on the backs of these giants. I might actually send each and every one of you a fruit basket this year.

Stop staring at me! I'm blank.

1 In the beginning

S pring was first introduced in March of 2004. I can remember sitting in a cramped auditorium in San Francisco listening to Rod Johnson explain how his little framework was going to stop the pain inflicted on us by the big fat application servers of that era. Actually, those fat application servers are every bit as ugly today, but I digress. Rod demonstrated how his Spring thingy was going to enable a more dynamic approach for modeling and coding enterprise applications. I sat there alongside my architect colleagues wondering what in the world Rod was even talking about. He went on to explain coupling and cohesion and interface-based modeling and we started looking at our watches to see if it was time for the free beer.

Little did I know, Spring would not only begin to make sense, but it would soon be adopted in nearly every enterprise-scale software product on the planet! Rod was a little ahead of the rest of us. Having worked several years at one company writing software for legacy IBM machinery and another decade climbing up the EE ladder at another, I have learned from a great many mistakes. I now have my own company where I get to tour the world teaching, lecturing and consulting on the right ways to design and implement lean and agile large-scale distributed IT solutions. Having the opportunity to work inside so many corporations has been both rewarding and challenging. One thing is for sure; they all face a similar set of obstacles:

- An over-complicated build environment
- Rarely adhered to or non-existent coding standards
- Testing? Who has time for that?
- Lack of formal education / training

Too busy mopping the floor to turn off the water!

It is time to turn off the water! With so much to do and so little time to do it, why not leverage Spring to look after all the mundane chores that we should have stopped doing years ago? Check this out -- a guy comes up to me last week in my Spring class and says "if I do this Spring thing, I'll lose my skills." I said "please do lose them, we need new ones." I followed up by telling him we make routine trips to the moon so why are we still writing all of the ridiculous code by hand that Spring already has shrink-wrapped into the framework.

This book series will discuss the good, the bad, and the ugly that we all encounter each day in this place we call "computer science." In reality it is more reminiscent of a murky technical debt swamp. At each turn along the way we will focus on Spring and how to leverage proven solutions to solve the whacky problems we find in our tar pits/corporations.

I chose to introduce Spring Next Generation as a series rather the one huge book for the following reasons:

- Spring is like a buffet line containing many modules and you should be allowed to pick and choose what you need
- By using a series of books, my goal is to keep the series version current as individual Spring modules are updated
- I am excited about the new version of Spring and want to put it in your hands as soon as possible
- Ultimately, I plan to use the series to deliver classroom training that is tailored to a particular client technology stack. Pick and choose what is needed from the series.

My plan is to begin making issues in the series available as quickly as I can crank them out. While I know most of you love reading the open source code, some of us would rather just read the book!

The first stop explores the core problem that Spring was designed to solve; reduce typing the **new()** operator in your source to the largest extent possible. I have traveled the world over the past couple of years as a consultant and educator and it is amazing to see how many shops do not get this simple concept.

1.1 The core problem

Most developers I talk to don't even understand the core problem Spring was designed to solve -- eliminate the stupid new() operator. When I ask engineers "what is the one thing we know about concrete" they typically respond with "it's hard". After acknowledging this fact, I tell them "it cracks and breaks." If we know concrete will break while we are pouring it, why would we even do it? Moreover, why would we pay so much money for something that will sometimes start breaking before it is even paid for? Using the new() operator is equivalent to pouring concrete into your application!

This is when developers will tell me "the only way to create an object in Java is by using the new keyword." While this is true (mostly) I respond by asking them why they are typing it in their source code at compile time. Nothing lasts for very long in modern software systems and it is a good bet that whatever objects are being created today will be superseded by better versions tomorrow. Obviously objects need to be created, but it is time for us to change our mindset about how and when to determine which object will be the best for the job.

I find that people enjoy analogies, so let's start off with a typical real world problem. You are heading off to start your day and need to strap on a pair of shoes. Which shoes do you grab? It depends, right? Is it raining or a hot sunny day? Are you going to work or is it the weekend? Perhaps you are on vacation in the mountains and heading for the ski lift. The shoes you grab will be determined by these and likely even additional factors such as which pair is the most comfortable.

It is obvious we have feet and shoes, so let's turn to Java and write some code.

```
1.  public class Person {
2.
3.      private Shoes shoes = new ??????();
4.
5.  }
```

Which shoes would you create on line 3?

- new BunnySlippers()
- new Boots()

Do you see the problem? We hardcode object creation in nearly every class we design. For some of us, we have been doing it for so long we are not even aware of the problems we are creating. While it is true that we need a new pair of shoes at some point, we should not be making assumptions about the best pair in a static and concrete compiled file!

So when would you know which is the best pair? What if you didn't need to decide at all, but rather, you had a personal assistant that found the best pair and placed them on your feet at just the right time? This personal assistant could check the weather forecast, your schedule of appointments for the day, your preferences over time and possibly text your friends. Perhaps you do not even own the most appropriate shoes, so your personal assistant runs to the store and purchases them. You simply look down at your feet with amazement and find that the best pair has been placed upon your feet.

Spring is that personal assistant! Spring was initially designed to provide the best possible object for us at the latest possible moment – real time. In OO speak, if a Person needs a pair of Shoes, Spring will inject that dependency for the Person. If this sounds like magic and you wonder how Spring could determine the best Shoes, take a deep breath and realize you are like everyone else. Developers freak out when they don't understand everything that is happening in a software application and I can totally understand this. How will we debug it? What about performance? Nobody can tell what the runtime behavior will be by simply looking at their code. Trust me, I've heard it all!

The truth of the matter is, we wouldn't make it through life as human beings if we were forced to understand how everything worked in this world. Think about it. You wouldn't be able to start your car without lifting the hood and knowing about all the bits. You couldn't operate a vending machine because you are not certain what happens when you slide your money into the slot. Let's face it, this abstraction of the world is the greatest thing ever! If you want to go up in an elevator you press the button and up you go. You don't need to know if it's cable and pulleys or hydraulically operated. Likewise, when you press the vending machine buttons E and 6 for that KitKat, the only thing you need to know is that it will be delicious.

1.2 A few design patterns & principles

Many of us believe that making an enhancement to an application starts with checking source code out of a repository. In fact, this has been the norm for so many years that it seems perfectly natural. Let us dispel this myth and consider the Open-Closed Principle. Software should be open for extension but closed to modification. What this means is we DO NOT begin with checking existing source code out of anything. We have all seen how an change to code results in a positive here and three other things now stop working over there.

This series of books will focus on a fictitious online everything store called lambazon.com. Our online everything store sells, well, everything. We will start off slow and work our way to rock stardom. Let's begin by looking at code we are all familiar with seeing today. This will allow us to perform side-by-side taste tests that illustrate the differences between old and new techniques. We will have orders, customers and everything imaginable for sale. We ship around the world and have merchants who market our everything as well. A customer has a status that is determined by their purchasing history and establishes their discounts and credit limits. Let us first consider a Customer and Status relationship modeled badly:

```
1.  package com.lambazon.domain;
2.
3.  public class Customer {
4.
5.      private Status status = Status.unset;
6.      private OrderHistory orderHistory = new OrderHistory();
7.
8.      public Customer() {
9.          determinePurchaseStatus();
10.     }
11.
12.     private void determinePurchaseStatus() {
13.         status = orderHistory.determineStatus(this);
14.     }
15.
16.     public Status getStatus() {
17.         return status;
18.     }
19. }
```

A Status works similar to a credit score and the purchasing history is responsible for its assignment. We see the Customer creating an object of type OrderHistory to use in determining its Status. Let's suppose there were business rules that determined how many months of sales should be included in the total. Also, what if we wanted to net returns against sales to come up with a more accurate purchase history? When we have such a variance in rules, the if/then/else logic can make understanding the application nearly impossible. Rather than tackle this the old way, let's stop for a moment and think about the big picture. It is not possible to see the forest with your face pressed up against a tree!

The Open-Closed Principle says we should be able to extend the application without modifying what exists now! This means we can change the runtime behavior to incorporate varying requirements without checking the existing code out at all. What the what? How can it work differently if we don't change existing code? If we begin by changing what is already running in production, there is a very high probability that we will suffer collateral damage. It's like Whack-A-Mole, but with bugs. You knock a bug out here and two new ones pop up over there. Every time you fix one bug you find you have broken something somewhere else.

Since the code we have now was written poorly, we will be forced to refactor it to work in the new way. The first thing we need to do is separate the *what* from the *how*. The *what* in our scenario is setting the customer Status based upon their purchasing history. The *how* should be unknown to the Customer source code. We know we need the Customer Status to be established but we DO NOT CARE HOW it is performed!

For those of us used to hard-coding this may be a radical departure so this is a good time to stop and reread that last paragraph until our breathing returns to normal. We will begin refactoring the Customer by creating an interface for the OrderHistory. An interface is the *what* and says nothing about *how* it will be performed. Objects implementing this interface will encapsulate *how* this is accomplished. Let's consider a few strategies we might want to use in computing the Customer Status.

1. Purchases made in the previous twelve months
2. Purchases for previous twelve months minus min./max Orders.
3. All purchases made except those that were returned

4. All purchases made excluding sale items

We haven't even considered seasonally adjusted purchases or accidental duplicate orders. In our new interface we accept a Customer and return the appropriate Status. Interface-based design is the most intelligent way to begin modeling an OO application – especially given the Java 8 flexibility.

```
1.  package com.lambazon.domain;
2.
3.  public interface OrderHistory {
4.
5.      public abstract Status determineStatus(Customer c);
6.
7.  }
```

Next let's eliminate using the new() keyword from the Customer:

```
1.  package com.lambazon.domain;
2.
3.  public class Customer {
4.
5.      private Status status = Status.unset;
6.      private OrderHistory orderHistory = null;
7.
8.      public Customer() {
9.          determinePurchaseStatus();
10.     }
11.
12.     private void determinePurchaseStatus() {
13.         status = orderHistory.determineStatus(this);
14.     }
15.
16.     public Status getStatus() {
17.         return status;
18.     }
19. }
```

Things are looking better, but now the Customer has no "real" OrderHistory object to use. In order to supply (or inject) an OrderHistory object into the Customer, we will now consider the Factory design pattern.

The Factory pattern models the idea of what a factory does in the real world. A factory takes in raw materials and produces finished goods. Think about a pair of shoes and a shoe factory. The factory takes in raw materials like, rubber, leather, string and other stuff and produces finished goods called shoes. Unless you work in the factory, chances are you have no idea how that construction worked or even who did what job. You simply asked for shoes and were able to strap them on your feet.

In software this is called loosely connected. The relationship you have with the shoe factory is very weak if you even consider it a coupling at all. The shoe factory could move their operation overseas and it wouldn't affect you. Heck you could move overseas and it wouldn't affect the shoe factory. This is the level of friction we would like between our "real world" objects inside our virtual machine object-oriented world.

We want the factory to provide the best possible version of its products and yet be largely independent of the consumers. This flexibility regarding the "best" version of the product is what we will soon discover makes our applications resilient and agile. As you will learn, Spring is the ultimate factory; we will start off slowly and explore, by hand, the mechanics of what a factory does. This will help us understand what Spring will soon be doing for us.

The following class reveals the factory design pattern. Notice how we use the generic get(Class<T> t) method to produce an object. We will not labor over that method because the brilliant folks who designed Spring have already wrestled that logic to the ground. This trivial factory is merely laid out here to illustrate the mechanics.

```
1.  package com.lambazon.factory;
2.
3.  import java.util.HashMap;
4.  import java.util.Map;
5.
6.  import com.lambazon.domain.OrderHistoryImpl;
7.
8.
9.  public class LambazonObjectFactory {
10.
11.     Map<String, Object> cache=new HashMap<String, Object>();
12.
13.        public static <T> T get(Class<T> t){
14.          // return best OrderHistory implementation here
15.          // If appropriate, we could cache the instance
16.        if (t==OrderHistory.class)
17.          return (T) new OrderHistoryImpl();
18.     }
19. }
```

Now we will add the factory reference to our Customer class so an OrderHistory implementation can be acquired. We are soon going to invert this dependency by removing the factory from the picture and simply satisfy the Customer need for an OrderHistory implementation. We will refer to this as the Hollywood Principle – "don't call us, we'll call you!". But for now, we see that the Customer is no longer hard coding any particular implementation of OrderHistory. If the factory wanted to supply a unique type because it happens to be a Saturday, then the factory can do this all without Customer ever knowing the difference. The Customer needs an OrderHistory, and that is precisely what it shall receive. Perfect!

```
1.   package com.lambazon.domain;
2.
3.   import com.lambazon.factory.LambazonObjectFactory;
4.
5.   public class Customer {
6.
7.       private Status status = Status.unset;
8.       private OrderHistory orderHistory =
9.               LambazonObjectFactory.get(OrderHistory.class);
10.
11.      public Customer() {
12.          determinePurchaseStatus();
13.      }
14.
15.      private void determinePurchaseStatus() {
16.          status = orderHistory.determineStatus(this);
17.      }
18.
19.      public Status getStatus() {
20.          return status;
21.      }
22. }
```

This design around interfaces combined with the factory design pattern has eliminated hardcoding anything into Customer and describes the core of what Spring provides us across our entire object application. You see, objects are being constructed, but not in our application code. The factory takes our raw goods in (objects) and produces finished products – objects fully wired up that are ready for use.

Now let's turn our attention to a modern technology stack for a typical application and ask the question: "what is an OO system anyway?"

2 What is an OO System

Many of us have experience in designing and writing software, however, that history may not line up well with Java and modern object oriented architectures. I worked with a large insurance company where we conducted lengthy boot camps to migrate programmers from legacy programming languages to Java. Programmers were expected to jettison decades of legacy programming skill and start doing things the OO way. But what does that even mean? I would lecture and the programmers would do lab exercises. In the beginning, their code resembled Jobol, a word I coined for describing what a Cobol programmer would write if they merely understood the mechanics of the Java programming language.

We would discuss their code and brainstorm techniques useful in refactoring it to be something that more resembled clean OO code. As it turned out, the word refactor was not even understood. After months of this back-and-forth I started to think the boot camp needed a prerequisite course that subtracted computers and programming languages and simply focused on where we were and what we were doing. Many of the programmers liked this approach and we started making real progress. I learned that what they were doing was using the skills they already had (duh) to solve the more difficult OO problems they had never faced before. They kept saying things like input, process and output. They were stuck in a procedural frame of mind and thinking top-down.

Once I realized where the mental disconnect was, I decided to go back in time and meet them halfway. I had been thinking in OO for so long I thought it was just well known; wrong-o. I decided to draw a picture on the board and discuss it. I chose a dog. Many people wondered if I had spun a bearing, however they were kind and allowed me to doodle. They wondered what a dog had to do with the insurance business and I told them it was a seeing eye dog used by a programmer. Hey, I had to try something here. I asked them what the doodle looked like to them and they stared strangely at me and said "a dog?" I doodled a purple cat next to the dog and asked what that doodle looked like. Again, strange looks followed by "a cat?" So I followed up by asking what the two had in common and they told me "nothing." See these were black & white programmers. One was a cat and the other a dog. I suppose they saw two different files or programs or some such procedural artifacts in their minds.

Aren't they both animals? What about mammals? Don't they both eat, sleep, poop and make sounds? What about a hamster? Is a hamster like the doodles I had drawn on the board? We were pointing at a couple mammals but seeing only a cat and a dog and not what they actually shared. I tried a slightly different approach since I was actually teaching the class and there were no animals in the room. I asked them what a teacher was and they sat there as if I had asked for the atomic weight of boron. One fellow pointed at me and said "you are." I asked if he knew other teachers and if they taught the same things I did. The exercise revealed a chasm between OO and the procedural world that existed before it.

In order to do OO correctly, you must first be able to think in objects. Without getting all bogged down in computer junk, what is an object? If you are sitting in a chair, that chair is an object. If you are holding this book in your hands it is an object, also. Heck, look around where you are right now and you will see hundreds if not thousands of objects. My desk, laptop, smart phone, coffee mug, guitar and even the room I'm working in are all objects. It would seem everything is an object of some type

So why is this useful? Before getting all scientific, ask yourself why an object having a name is useful. Without naming things, how could we communicate about them? As I write this morning there is frozen rain coming down from the sky in the form of fluffy white things. What if we had no word to describe a snowflake? See what I mean? Is rain the same as snow as it relates to precipitation? We will ponder this sort of abstraction in much greater detail.

So an object has a name and can be classified into some categorical mental "food group" in your mind. If I say shoe or guitar you can quickly get the gist of what these object types are without another word being spoken. If you ask about my car I might say it's a 2014 Chevrolet Corvette Stingray

Now let's expand on this notion of a car. We see it is a beautiful car that happens to also fall into the category of a high-performance sports car. We can also see it has only two doors and seats two passengers. What other objects come to mind as you look at this car? Depending on your experience with a car, you could easily write a book about all the objects that go into the design and development of this Corvette. I'll list a few just to get the mind lubricated:

- Manufacturer
- Power source (engine, battery, etc.)
- Transmission
- Wheels
- Tires
- Starter motor
- Entertainment system
- Interior
- Exhaust
- Carbon fiber exterior
- Glass roof
- Instrument cluster
- Drivetrain

In OO speak, a car is actually an abstract type of object. Think about it this way, if you were to unscrew all the bolts and screws and break every wire weld, you would be left with a pile of parts. A car is the composition of its parts assembled in a meaningful way. Think about an assembly line where many people and robots worked to "build" the car from the parts so you can drive it. A car without its engine would not be very useful.

Let's take this notion of object composition and OO to the next level.

2.1 The object

If you consider just about any object for a moment, you will discover it is probably composed of other objects. We saw a car was really just the assembly of many related parts. This is what we call object composition in OO parlance. Think about yourself in this context. You are a composition of many bones making up your skeleton, internal organs and maybe some really cool hair! So if you contain a heart does that mean you are a heart? Of course not. It only means you have a heart. This is the bedrock of object modeling; determining what objects make up your problem domain and assigning each of them a name. The relationships between objects are much like the ERD's we have been looking at for decades. The big difference between object modeling and entity-relationship-diagrams is that OO modeling does not involve a database or tables. In fact this is a great time to subtract programs and files from your thinking. Those are artifacts of years gone by; like the cassette tape player.

So if everything revolves around objects and objects are composed of other related objects, let's take a few minutes and shine a flashlight inside an object. An object is typically a noun (person, place, or thing) but can also be synthesized to play the role of a verb. Don't get too hung up on this right now; just make sure you name your objects something to which a human being could relate. I've seen some crazily named objects that were a relic of some stupid programming standard. A name like RN_133X that was in fact a registered nurse object. When asked why the heck a name like that was chosen for a RegisteredNurse, I got this blank stare and a bunch of jibber jabber about old program naming standard; stop the crazy!

An object is the digital representation of a thing. These objects are the real-world replicas realized in the virtual world and we cannot actually see or touch them, right? So how can we interact with them and how do they interact with each other? They respond to messages! If you want to know the temperature where you are, you could send the weather object a message like "hey weather object, what is the temperature for postal code 62025?" I just asked and the answer is minus 4 Fahrenheit / -20 Celsius. An object communicates with other objects by exchanging messages and an object may contain only properties and behaviors. This simple definition is technically as complicated as it gets. Seriously!

Let's open up our weather object and have a look inside. We notice it has a name, three properties and three behaviors:

```
1.    package com.lambazon.domain;
2.
3.    public class Weather {
4.
5.        // properties
6.        private double temperatureAsCelsius;
7.        private Internet www = new Internet();
8.        private String url = "weather.com?zipCode=";
9.
10.       //behaviors
11.       public String whatIsTheTemperature(String zipCode){
12.           temperatureAsCelsius = www.webService(url+zipCode);
13.
14.           return "The temperature for " +
15.                   zipCode +
16.                   " is " +
17.                   asFahrenheit() +
18.                   " F and " +
19.                   asCelsius() +
20.                   " C";
21.       }
22.
23.       private double asCelsius(){
24.           return temperatureAsCelsius;
25.       }
26.
27.       private double asFahrenheit(){
28.           return (temperatureAsCelsius*9)/5 + 32;
29.       }
30.
31. }
```

We see the name of the class is Weather. This is a great name for an object that can tell you the temperature. One might argue that thermometer would be a better name, but we can leave that for another page. The three properties are an internal floating point variable to hold the temperature as Celsius, a reference to an Internet object for the web service call and a String for the base weather service url. Notice that of the three behaviors, only one can actually be accessed outside the weather object itself.

So the published weather API (application programming interface) that we expose to the world allows a client to send it the single message whatIsTheTemperature(zip) and it responds by returning the temperature as a String.

```
The temperature for 62025 is -4.0 F and -20.0 C
```

We pass the weather object a message and it magically responds with the temperature. How did it figure out what the temperature was? Look back and see if there were any objects to which the weather object might have sent a message. Notice the weather object is sending a message to an Internet object to actually determine the temperature for our requested zip code. Our weather object understands how to perform this web service call and also perform Celsius to Fahrenheit conversions.

But why two objects? An object oriented system is always composed of objects but determining the number of objects is not a science. In this case, I did not own a weather station so I had no way to determine the temperature. A quick Google search revealed a web service on the internet I could use to fetch the temperature. So my weather object has a relationship with an Internet object that actually makes the web service call.

This separation of concerns is a critical aspect to building a versatile and agile application. We have separated the what from the how. We have no idea how that web service call determines the temperature for us. This will become a theme throughout all of your OO career. **We don't know the how and furthermore, we don't care.** If a better, faster, cheaper way to determine the temperature comes along tomorrow (and it will) we change over to use it and the rest of our application simply works a little better, faster and cheaper, all without changing it! Sweetness.

So if someone asks you "what is an OO system?" You can tell them it is a network of interacting objects where the interaction is simply the passing of messages. In the next section we will explore this subject in a little more detail.

2.2 The messages

Have you ridden a bicycle with gears? Have you changed the gears? If you said yes, look at your hands to see if they are greasy and bloody. If they are not, you will discover you did not change the gears, the bike did. You merely sent a message to your bicycle asking it to change its gears. If you had changed the gears, you would have probably wrecked your bike leaning toward the ground while pedaling. Moreover, what to do with that bicycle chain? Do you move it on the front or rear sprocket and to which cog? If you had to actually know how to change the ratio of pedal rotation relative to ground speed, you would probably leave it in one gear all the time and suffer up the hills.

Again, we see the what and the how come into play. *What* you want to do is have the bicycle in a lower gear for that hill up ahead, but *how* the gear change occurs is none of your concern. If you think back to the earlier discussion between Customer Status and OrderHistory, you will recall we separated the what from the how by introducing interfaces alongside classes. In this section we will discuss message passing between types and the relationship between objects, interfaces, classes and types. Remember that an object communicates with other objects by exchanging messages and an object may contain only properties and behaviors.

Java is a strongly typed object language which means every object you encounter will be of some type -- Dog, Bicycle, Order, etc. Moreover, a type of object has a well-defined public interface or published API. The published interface is the service(s) an object can provide to other objects. Let's consider the Order type from our online everything store, lambazon.

```
1.  package com.lambazon.domain;
2.
3.  import java.util.Collection;
4.
5.  public class Order {
6.
7.      //properties
8.      private Customer customer;
9.      private Collection<Item> orderItems;
10.
11.     //behaviors
12.     public void add(Item item){ }
13.     public void remove(Item item){ }
14.     public double total(){ return 0.0; }
15. }
```

The Order is the essential object type for the business, and as such serves a pivotal role in the object model. In the spirit of brevity, Order contains only a reference to its Customer and a Collection of the items on the Order. Also, the behaviors are stubbed at the moment and do not contain valid instructions. These object references are those related to Order. They are said to have a relationship with Order in the object model. These relationships establish a connection between the types whereby messages flow. Let us suppose we would like to know the order total for the customer. We have already discussed how a Customer has a related Status which determines the pricing rules.

If we were to send Order the message asking for the total, we can see the first thing Order would have to do is send a message to its Customer asking for the associated Status. A Status of gold will result in better discounts than silver. Additionally, if you recall the way Customer determines the Status, you will find another relationship between the Customer and OrderHistory types.

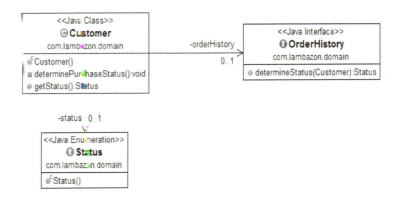

Wow! This is pretty confusing now. I'm not sure why we have so many objects anyway. Couldn't we just put all the Java code in one class and call it JOBOL? The reason this looks so different from that monolithic structured program you have been poking at for a few decades is because it models the real world and not some top-down language where you kept typing source code until you reached the million line mark. Nobody could understand that mess; not even you!

Object-oriented applications are all about the real world, so let's discuss that for a moment. Look at the following picture and write down what you see in a single word.

If you are like most, you wrote down the word trees. There are clearly many different types of trees in this picture. Some are flowering and others may bear fruit. I see tall trees, short trees, old trees and new. I see trees that hardly look like trees; maybe they are shrubs or bushes. Some are deciduous and others evergreen. Some might even be poisonous!

With so many differences, how can we see the word tree immediately upon seeing this photo? In object speak we call this an abstraction. If we didn't have abstraction in this world, I don't think we'd make it far. Suppose you need to rent a car for a trip. You are prompted to describe what type of car you need and you say it doesn't matter. You could be handed keys to a car, truck, jeep or crossover vehicle, right? You asked for a car because you have mentally generalized all vehicles this way.

In the object world we will do this same thing. Getting back to lambazon.com and the OrderHistory, we see this in action. OrderHistory is the tree which is an abstract type. The particular species of OrderHistory types are each self-contained objects that play the role of an OrderHistory type. In order to see things graphically, consider the following class diagram which illustrates several key elements and we will discuss them each:

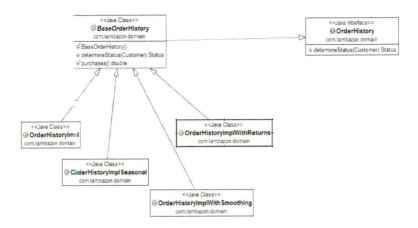

- OrderHistory interface
- BaseOrderHistory abstract class
- OrderHistory implementations

We will start off by considering the OrderHistory interface -- this is our *what* and as such contains *no how* (code).

```
1. package com.lambazon.domain;
2.
3. public interface OrderHistory {
4.
5.     public abstract Status determineStatus(Customer c);
6.
7. }
```

While it is simply an interface, it is 100% a type in the Java language. Remember, Java is a strongly typed object language, so every object must be of some type. Most of the time you will not even realize you are dealing with an interface. It's simply a type in a type system. In fact, if you have worked with JDBC and the Statement, Connection and ResultSet types, you may be surprised to know those were all interfaces!

So what is the value of this interface? It allows us to future-proof our application. Did you catch that? FUTURE-PROOF BABY! Look below at Customer and notice to which OrderHistory implementation it is bound.

```
1.  package com.lambazon.domain;
2.
3.
4.  public class Customer {
5.
6.      private Status status = Status.unset;
7.      private OrderHistory orderHistory;
8.
9.      private void determinePurchaseStatus() {
10.         status = orderHistory.determineStatus(this);
11.     }
12.
13. }
```

The Customer is not bound to any concrete (how) implementation at all! It simply refers to a related OrderHistory type which just so happens to be a trivial little interface. This means we can provide Customer any one of the four ways to calculate order history. If the business determines we need a fifth way to determine purchase history, we simply add another OrderHistoryImplFifthWay and we never tamper with the Customer at all. Brilliant! The next type we examine is the BaseOrderHistory.

```
1.    package com.lambazon.domain;
2.
3.    public abstract class BaseOrderHistory implements OrderHistory {
4.
5.        public Status determineStatus(Customer customer) {
6.
7.            double purchases = purchases();
8.
9.            if (purchases <= 100) {
10.               return Status.Red;
11.           } else if (purchases <= 1000) {
12.               return Status.Green;
13.           } else if (purchases <= 10000) {
14.               return Status.Silver;
15.           } else if (purchases <= 100000) {
16.               return Status.Gold;
17.           } else {
18.               return Status.Titanium;
19.           }
20.       }
21.
22.       public abstract double purchases();
23. }
```

BaseOrderHistory is an abstract class, which only means
we cannot create an object of that type directly. This class
implements the OrderHistory interface which means
BaseOrderHistory is an OrderHistory type. I added this
class because the logic to determine the Customer Status is
a fixed function of total purchases and should not be
duplicated among the OrderHistory implementations.
Notice the abstract method:

```
22.       public abstract double purchases();
```

This method is marked abstract and so it contains no code.
This will require the actual OrderHistory implementations
to override it and provide the actual total purchases using
its unique logic. The real OrderHistory implementation
classes are the different strategies we use when determining
a Customer's total purchases. I'll list only a couple of them,
since they are structurally alike, only their logic differs.

```
1.   package com.lambazon.domain;
2.
3.   public class OrderHistoryImplWithSmoothing extends BaseOrderHistory {
4.
5.       /*
6.        * This logic applies exponential smoothing
7.        */
8.       public double purchases() {
9.           //TODO
10.          return 0.0;
11.      }
12.
13. }
```

```
1.   package com.lambazon.domain;
2.
3.   public class OrderHistoryImplWithReturns extends BaseOrderHistory {
4.
5.       /*
6.        * This logic factors returns against purchases
7.        */
8.       public double purchases() {
9.           //TODO
10.          return 0.0;
11.      }
12.
13. }
```

Whew! This is starting to make a little more sense now. I'm starting to see how the parts fit together, but I'm still not sure how that Customer is going to have one of those OrderHistory objects wired up. Moreover, who is going to decide the right one and when? This is a great place to stop and reflect. I'm heading out for Indian food and I suggest you place a bookmark here and we'll meet up after I've had my naan.

3 Organizing the Objects

Now that we have a good idea about classes, objects, interfaces and abstraction, let's discuss how to organize the objects. I realize you want to jump in and begin finishing up the Customer, but we need to come up with a blueprint for our technology stack first. If you want your application to scale to the tune of millions of transactions per second, partitioning your objects across many machines in a server farm is essential business. It is typical to have hundreds or even thousands of servers running your application and realizing this ahead of time will pay huge dividends later on.

Just like we do not put all of our clothes in a single drawer (where are my socks?) we will not put all of our objects in a single place either. Moreover, as we put frozen items in our freezer and others like milk, eggs, and beer below in the refrigerator, so too will we put related groupings of objects into separate compartments. This will provide many benefits, including the possibility of placing specific groups of objects on particular server machines that are tuned best for their targeted purpose.

As we get deeper into developing and wiring the objects

together, you will be happy we took this pause.

3.1 The technology stack

We will have many different types of objects in our lambazon.com OO application and we need to sort out how we plan on packaging them up before starting to write code. Much can be gained by looking at the big picture and deciding what types of objects will go where. Our application will have a Spring MVC web front end and also be exposed via Spring RESTful web services. We will use Spring transaction managers and JPA (Java Persistence API) for object persistence. In addition we will incorporate a full host of Spring modules like Batch, Integration, Social, Remote access, Security, Aspects, etc.

The first thing I like to do is establish the tiers appropriate for my technology stack and determine how many projects, modules and artifacts will be required. I have tried wrapping this all up in a single application and it never works out well in practice. Let's consider a typical stack before continuing.

Domain Model	Security
	Cache/Queue/Replicate/Localization
	Controller
	Service
	Repository
	Persistence
	Integration
	Batch

We see the top of the stack is the security layer. This is the gatekeeper and prevents unauthorized access. As we work our way down the stack, we ultimately traverse all the layers and return a response to the requester. The domain model contains the business objects and supplies the model (data) across the tiers. This is the layer I typically start with since it is the core of the application.

Another key benefit of the technology stack design is separation of concerns. Thinking back to **what** vs. **how**, we see layers in the stack responsible for a particular role in the request and response lifecycle. For instance, the persistence layer is responsible for saving our object graphs to a non-volatile store. However, nowhere does this blueprint suggest how this is going to happen. Perhaps it is using a hosted relational data store. Maybe it uses Amazon buckets or some such cloud storage. By separating *what* needs to be performed from *how* to do it, we can more easily switch from one strategy to another in a single place. Lastly, you will soon discover how Spring allows you to apply "special sauce" to a grouping or layer of objects. The special sauce might be adding support for cache, transactional behaviors or where to apply aspects. Having partitioned our application in layers will allow us to easily activate this special functionality.

In the next section we will begin to focus on the domain layer and core business objects.

3.2 The domain model

The domain model is likely the most stable part of a software application and it is where you identify the major parts of the object model. We are talking about the primary reason you are writing the software in the first place! For lambazon.com, it's all about creating orders for customers and packing, billing and shipping the orders.

We will start off with the most common use case where a Customer places an Order for Items. Clearly, these object types are entities (JPA Persistent types) and need to be saved and also accessible up and down the technology stack. We chose com.lambazon as our base package name and will tack on as many sub-namespaces as we have layers and functionality across the application. In order to prepare for development we will create the following package names as a starting point:

- com.lambazon.domain
- com.lambazon.security
- com.lambazon.cache
- com.lambazon.queue
- com.lambazon.replication
- com.lambazon.localization
- com.lambazon.controller
- com.lambazon.service
- com.lambazon.repository
- com.lambazon.persistence
- com.lambazon.integration
- com.lambazon.batch

This will give us packaged name spaces for our objects and also help nudge us in the right direction along the way. If we are writing a service class and notice a package called com.lambazon.service, we'll probably end up putting the new class in the right place! This might sound trivial, but you would be surprised at the messy applications I have seen. Something as simple as packaging your types according to the role they play will pay enormous dividends during the life of the application.

Our order and its related domain objects can be found in the com.lambazon.domain package. The following class diagram illustrates the first pass at these core associated objects:

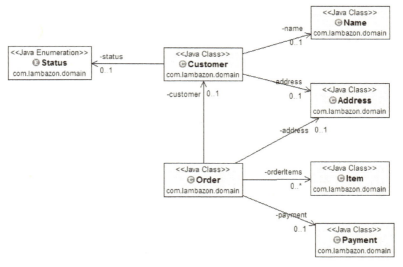

These are the object types that need to be accessible from many different layers in the stack. Also, realizing that different layers may reside on dissimilar machinery, the only real requirement we might have is that these types be serializable to allow for distributed and remote access.

The next section will focus on the messages passed along the object chain and how we can substitute technology choices quickly and easily.

3.3 Message sequencing

Okay, so we have roughed out a few domain types which will allow a customer to create an order for lambazon.com. In addition, we have established some structure and organization for the application by creating a technology stack. So what objects will be required to create an order and where will they go? This can be explained fairly easily without much knowledge of the bits and bytes behind the curtain. A software application exists for one reason -- to provide answers to questions! Think about this for a second, it doesn't matter if it is an old COBOL program running an insurance company or a shiny new mobile app you use to make dinner reservations. You have questions and the software provides the answers.

Sometimes I wonder how we ordered anything before the internet or online existed. Did we have to call someone or drive to a store? Were we all just writing things down on a notebook? Yes, and the computer only streamlines and makes this more efficient.

At the moment we have a technology stack awaiting a request to come in at the top and then each successive layer participates in determining what answer will ultimately be returned to the requester. We will refer to this generically as the request-response cycle.

We will receive many different requests and need to respond to each one in a request-sensitive way. Let's identify a few requests we can imaging receiving at lambazon.com:

- Create a new customer
- Modify an existing customer
- Create a payment method
- Place an order
- Modify an order
- Search for an order
- Determine customer status by totaling their order history
- Ship an order
- Process a customer return

The controller, service and repository layers provide us with patterns useful in responding to requests. Let's stop and see what we mean by this. A controller is typically where a request is first considered. If we look back at the list of potential requests we expect, we might realize the following controllers need to be available.

- CustomerController
- OrderController
- PaymentController
- ShippingController

The controller will have minimal responsibility and exists largely to provide a starting point for responding to a request. This is where we may find first level validation and language conversions. The one thing that is certain is our controller will hand this request off to the appropriate service by passing the request message down the stack.

We see a symmetry between the controller, service and repository types:

- CustomerService
- OrderService
- PaymentService
- ShippingService

A service will perform the heavy lifting and usually message other controllers in the process. The service layer is not concerned with what type of requester made the call. It could be a human using a web browser, another machine (B2B), or a mobile device – the service layer does not care.

The service enforces the business rules and accounts for most of the requirements of the application. Finally, our service will pass requests off to the appropriate repository by passing messages down the stack:

- CustomerRepository
- OrderRepository
- PaymentRepository
- ShippingRepository

The next section will discuss techniques for creating a clean API (Application Programming Interface) that will allow easy plug-n-play of the technologies involved in the various layers of our technology stack.

3.4 A common vocabulary

With our domain model in place and the request-response cycle under our belts, let's consider an API that will allow a transparent messaging scheme between the controller, service and repository layers of our technology stack. We know a request will go through these three layers in that order and now need to identify what the message passing will look like.

Java Generic types give us new possibilities so let's clarify how they work. If you have used the java.util framework, you have undoubtedly seen these guys before. Generics were added to the language to add stability to your code by detecting certain programming bugs at compile time. We will create our own generic types for lambazon.com to allow us to design a clean and simple API.

Okay, so we have roughed out a few domain types that should allow a customer to create an order for lambazon.com. In addition, we have established some structure and organization for the application by creating a technology stack. So let's look at a possible API.

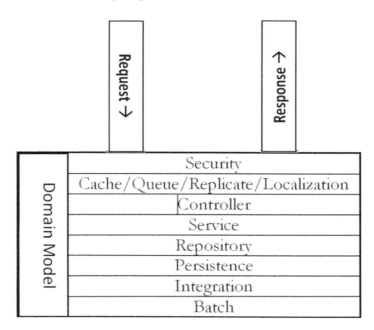

We start off by creating a generic interface for each of the three layers. This will allow generic types to be switched into the controller, service and repository types. Consider the generic controller below:

```
1.  public interface Controller<T> {
2.
3.      public T get(int id);
4.      public Collection<T> getAll(Class<T> t);
5.      public Collection<T> getFiltered(Class<T> t, Criteria criteria);
6.      public T save(T t);
7.      public T remove(T t);
8.
9.  }
```

This permits us to create generic controllers for any domain type. Below we create three controllers which can be dealt with in a uniform way. Any one looks exactly like another. Keep in mind that we might have additional interfaces beyond this core API. Also, if we need to add new messages to an existing interface, Java 8 is going to allow this more easily with the introduction of functional interfaces and virtual extension methods.

```
1.  private Controller<Customer> customerController;
2.
3.  private Controller<Order> orderController;
4.
5.  private Controller<Payment> paymentController;
```

Now that we see the mechanics of the API, let's review the customer controller, service and repository types and consider a typical message flow.

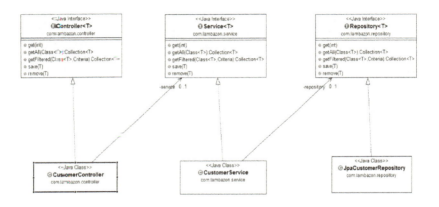

This is interface-based design at its finest! We have no concrete classes being referenced, only generic interface types. So how will we save an Order? orderController.save(anOrder). What about saving a Customer? customerController.save(aCustomer). But how do those two methods work? Do you really care? If they work isn't that good enough? If you are bored you could go look at the concrete classes. However, those may not be the real classes that do the work next week. It's called evolution baby.

The following sequence diagram illustrates the sequence of messages that result in running the TestCustomer Junit test case. The test creates a customer controller and asks it for a customer:

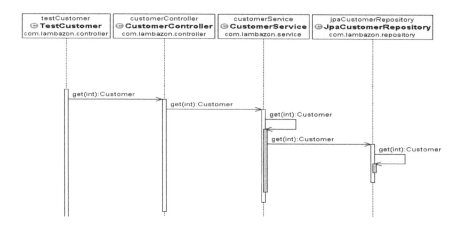

You will notice each successive message call, returns the customer that was ultimately constructed inside the innermost JpaCustomerRepository. Moreover, this sequence of messages does not indicate local or remote access.

This traversal of messages is called the Delegation Pattern and it is where engineers tend to begin raising their hands. They will ask why three different types with the same APIs? Isn't that a bad design? I like to get engineers thinking for themselves, so I will ask them if they believe it would be better to have fewer layers, remembering that each layer plays a particular role in the technology stack and may not be deployed to the same machinery. The usual response is that we *should* have the three layers. So I ask what the API should look like for each layer. Should they be different? What do you think? The generically typed domain object that is being passed up and down the stack is of the object type with all the unique behaviors! Specifically, Controller<**Customer**> Controller<**Order**>. Customer can be sent messages it understands and Order will clearly have a unique API as well.

This design aspect really is an exciting piece of working on an OO application. It is more an art and less a science. However, I find certain designs are more enjoyable to work with in practice.

Finally, recall these generic interfaces define only the message name and not how that operation will be performed. Think about it this way, a business user can ask the controller to get the customer with identifier 123 and that customer will be returned. The fact that this controller consulted with a service, which in turn consulted with a repository is simply an implementation detail.

In the next section we will look at how we can easily swap one technology implementation for another. This is the plug-n-play that will allow our OO application to evolve at the speed of change.

3.5 Thinking in USB

Now we have layered our application into a technology stack and have started roughing up a use case for creating an order, let's step back a moment and consider the plug-n-play metaphor. Moreover, let's discuss the universal serial bus and why it is so successful.

The reason USB is so successful is the fact you can truly plug a gadget in and it just works. The gadget could be a camera, hard drive smart phone or headphones and the connection is understood. I liken this to LEGO® bricks.

LEGO® bricks are interchangeable. You can plug-n-play LEGO®s for hours building a masterpiece and easily change a piece later on without breaking anything. As long as the new piece is the same shape (USB) as the old brick, it could be made from any material and be any color.

So what does this have to do with our lambazon.com application? Let's suppose our application is running in production and customers are coming from every corner of the planet to place their orders. We are so successful that we have outgrown the limits of our original design decisions. Let's suppose we had been using an Oracle database and have now exceeded our response time SLA (service level agreement). We need to swap the relational database for a Big Data solution. Remember that our controller, service and repository layers all conform to a uniform API (interface) so the parts are already implementation agnostic. This means the layers don't even know we are using Oracle now! The following class diagram reveals this by showing the actual relationships between the layers:

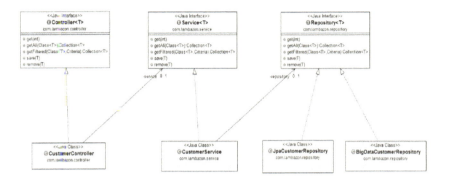

If you noticed we have no concrete class depending on any other concrete class, you just earned yourself a gold star! If we want to replace our repository implementation with a big data style, we do not tamper with existing code. We simply add the BigDataCustomerRepository.

So now you have to be wondering when and who decides the particular classes that are created and further what determines the way they get wired up to related objects. If we are no longer creating objects ourselves with the new() operator, then how will objects be created at all?

We started off this series by discussing the little framework called Spring that entered the scene back in 2004. Mr. Rod demonstrated how you could write better code if you stopped pouring concrete in your objects and instead turned object management over to Spring. In volume 2 of this Spring Next Generation series, we will explore the ultimate factory we call the Spring **Core Container.**

ABOUT THE AUTHOR

As an author speaker, musician and software architect, Scott Stanlick is a colorful dude. Scott has been instrumental inside IT shops ranging in size from a few million to many billions of dollars in revenue. He educates in the application of new technologies at universities and corporations around the world and also consults with industry. He enjoys motorcycling and considers people skills his greatest strength.

www.ingramcontent.com/pod-product-compliance
Lightning Source LLC
Chambersburg PA
CBHW031231050326
40689CB00009B/1552